From Questions to Communion: Discovering Catholicism

John H Brennan

Published by John H Brennan, 2024.

FROM QUESTIONS TO COMMUNION: DISCOVERING CATHOLICISM

First edition. June 1, 2024.

ISBN: 979-8224571710

Written by John H Brennan.

In Thanksgiving for all the wonderful Christian men and women of all Denominations who have lovingly challenged my own Catholic Faith over the years to choose it as my vehicle into the Promised Land.

John, the Pilgrim

Introduction: Embarking on a Journey

Welcome, dear reader, to a journey of discovery—a journey that begins with questions and leads to communion. Whether you come from a Protestant background, or from a different faith tradition altogether, this book invites you to explore the rich tapestry of Catholicism with an open mind and a willing heart.

Even for some of us who grew up inside the Catholic Faith, the rituals, sacraments, and traditions of Catholicism can seem mysterious, even daunting. Some of us learned it and forgot, some of us never really learned it in the first place! Some of us may have become disillusioned because of a priest or nun and decided to try something else, or nothing at all. In any case, there is so much about what happens within the walls of Catholic Churches around the country, and indeed, around the world that seems mysterious.

We may have questions about why Catholics do what they do, and how these practices connect to their faith and beliefs. We may wonder about the saints, the Mass, the veneration of Mary, and so much more.

In this book, we embark on a journey to find answers to these questions. But more than that, we embark on a journey of discovery—a journey of understanding, appreciation, and perhaps even transformation.

Lawrence grew up in an Evangelical Christian family and held many misconceptions about the Catholic faith. He viewed it through a lens clouded by hearsay, misunderstanding, and sometimes even prejudice.

Lawrence was on his way to a doctor's appointment about an hour from home. He had never been to this doctor, but his own primary care physician recommended to him to get a second option about a procedure he would be having in about a month. He set his GPS for the doctor's office and away he went.

It was a particularly hot summer day, so he had the air conditioning cranked up and was listening to Casting Crowns, Chris Brown, Chris Tomlin and many others. These songs were uplifting and were a perfect way for Lawrence to hand over his health concerns to the Lord and not to worry about the future.

As he pulled off the highway, the GPS directed him around an accident on the original route and was now headed through a residential suburban neighborhood. His car engine suddenly started sputtering, making knocking and hissing sounds. A parking lot was about 50 feet ahead, so he pulled in to assess the problem.

With the hood up, he went to work, trying to figure out what was wrong with his car. The sun was beating down on his back and he quickly realized that he was over his head with diagnosing the problem. He called the doctor's office and said he was having car troubles and would have to reschedule his appointment.

Lawrence heard people talking behind him and realized that it was a church parking lot and there was a funeral which just finished. The casket was loaded into the hearse and the procession of cars left for the cemetery.

Shortly after that, a man walked up to Lawrence and introduced himself, saying he was the altar server for the funeral Mass that had just ended and he noticed that Lawrence needed help. He listened to the engine and said that it sounded like the fuel injection system had become clogged, preventing gasoline from getting to the cylinders for combustion. Apparently, James had his own car repair shop and happened to have driven his tow-truck to church that day to assist in the funeral Mass.

James explained that he could tow Lawrence's car to his shop and be back with it in an hour or so. The passenger seat of his truck had parts on it that he rebuilt at home and he couldn't bring Lawrence to the shop, so he suggested Lawrence slip into the back of church and use the bathroom to clean up a bit and stay cool in the air conditioning at the church. James assured Lawrence that it most likely was the injectors and would only be labor and he wouldn't charge anything for labor for a stranded Christian.

This book is born out of that journey—a journey of exploration, conversation, and enlightenment as a result of where God placed Lawrence, as painful as the disruption was in his day. It is a testament to the belief that understanding breeds empathy, and empathy fosters unity. While Lawrence believed theological differences existed, there is much we can learn from one another, and much we can gain by walking together in dialogue and respect.

Throughout these pages, we will encounter the beauty and complexity of Catholicism. We will explore the significance of sacraments, the lives of saints, the power of prayer, and the richness of Catholic traditions. We will delve into the Roman Catholic Mass—the central act of Catholic worship—and uncover its layers of meaning and symbolism.

Centuries of growing division have led to anger, resentment, and misunderstanding. This is the time, we all should seek communion—not only within the Christian Community but with one another, as fellow seekers on the journey of faith. For in the end, our shared belief in eternal salvation through Jesus Christ binds us together more closely than our differences divide us.

So, let us embark on this journey together. Let us set aside preconceptions and stereotypes, and open our hearts to the wisdom and beauty that awaits us.

Let us journey from questions to communion, guided by curiosity, humility, and the Wisdom of the Holy Spirit for mutual respect.

May this book be a beacon of light on your path, illuminating the treasures of Catholicism, why Catholics love the traditions of

Catholicism and inspiring a deeper understanding of our shared journey of faith.

Welcome, and may our journey together be blessed.

The Entrance and the Holy Water Font

Lawrence stood outside the imposing structure of St. Michael's Catholic Church, his skepticism apparent in his furrowed brow. A lifelong Evangelical Christian, Lawrence had always viewed Catholic practices with suspicion. He believed their ways of worship, prayers, sacraments, and sacramentals were not truly based in Scripture but were rather misguided traditions developed over centuries.

James had suggested I walk in through the doors in the front of the church to clean the dirt from my car off my hands and relax for an hour or so while James fixed his car. As the heavy wooden doors creaked open, Lawrence couldn't help but notice the distinct scent of incense lingering in the air. Was this what a Catholic Church smelled like or was it a residual scent from the Funeral Mass which had just finished?

Lawrence noticed a small bowl of water in a recess in the wall as he walked in, one on either side wall of the vestibule to the church. Bewildered as to the purpose of the bowls of water, he stood there wondering if this was where James had suggested he wash his hands.

As Lawrence stood there, Father Matt, one of the parish priests, walked across the entrance to the church from the vestibule, catching a glimpse of someone standing in front of the Holy Water Font. Father stopped and welcomed Lawrence with a warm smile, ready to shake hands as he introduced himself and asked if he could help with something. Lawrence quickly showed Father Matt his hands and responded that his car broke down and James took his car to his shop for a repair. Lawrence said that James suggested to go inside the church and wash his hands, but didn't know where the washroom was. Father

Matt showed Lawrence the men's room as Lawrence revealed that he was an Evangelical Christian and admitted he had never been in a Catholic Church before.

Father Matt waited outside the restroom and prayed to the Holy Spirit for guidance to make this chance encounter be fruitful for both of them. As Lawrence emerged from the restroom, he said to Father Matt that his hands were now clean and he would take that handshake now.

"Welcome, Lawrence," Father Matt said, his voice gentle yet firm. "I'm glad you're here. Would you like to explore the church? I have a free afternoon and it's in the upper 90's outside today. You are free to just wait here or I could give you a tour and try to answer any questions you may have about what you see or anything about the Catholic faith."

Lawrence nodded, trying to keep an open mind. "Thanks, Father Matt. I'm curious to see what this is all about."

Lawrence said he would really appreciate a tour and said he wanted to know right off the bat, what the bowls of water he saw as he stepped inside the church and led Father Matt to the Holy Water Font. Intrigued but skeptical, he glanced at Father Matt for a response.

"This is a Holy Water font," Father Matt explained. "It's usually placed near the entrances of a Catholic church."

Lawrence peered into the font, puzzled. "Holy Water? What's it for? Is it really necessary?"

Father Matt smiled, anticipating the question. "Holy Water is water that has been blessed by a priest. It's a sacramental, which means it's a sacred sign that helps prepare us to receive God's grace. Catholics use it to remind themselves of their baptism and to seek spiritual cleansing and protection."

"Sounds a bit superstitious to me," Lawrence muttered, crossing his arms.

"Let me show you something," Father Matt said, dipping his fingers into the Holy Water. He then made the Sign of the Cross, touching his forehead, chest, left shoulder, and right shoulder. "In the name of the Father, and of the Son, and of the Holy Spirit."

Lawrence watched carefully. "So, what does this Sign of the Cross mean?"

"The Sign of the Cross is a way to acknowledge and honor the Holy Trinity—God the Father, God the Son, and God the Holy Spirit," Father Matt explained. "It's also a physical prayer asking for God's blessing and protection. It's a beautiful way to start and end prayers and to remind ourselves of our faith."

Lawrence frowned slightly. "But where is that in the Bible?"

"While the specific gesture of the Sign of the Cross isn't detailed in the Bible, the concept of the Trinity is biblical," Father Matt replied, "In Matthew 28:19, Jesus instructs His disciples to baptize 'in the name of the Father and of the Son and of the Holy Spirit.' The Sign of the Cross is a reflection of that command."

As Father Matt spoke, Lawrence noticed a subtle sense of reverence in his actions. It wasn't just a ritual—it was a deeply personal act of faith.

"Okay, but what about the water itself?" Lawrence asked. "Why water?"

"Water is a powerful symbol in Christianity," Father Matt explained. "It signifies purity and the washing away of sin. Just as water cleanses our bodies, Holy Water is a reminder that God cleanses our souls. It's a tangible reminder of our baptism and God's grace."

Lawrence paused, contemplating this new perspective. "I never thought of it that way. It always seemed like just another tradition."

"Every tradition in the Catholic Church has deep spiritual significance," Father Matt said gently. "They're not just rituals; they're ways to connect more deeply with our faith and God's love for us."

As they moved further into the church, the soft light filtering through stained glass windows cast colorful patterns on the floor. Lawrence felt a small shift in his heart. Perhaps there was more to these Catholic practices than he had previously understood.

"Thank you for explaining this, Father Matt," Lawrence said, a hint of gratitude in his voice. "I'm looking forward to learning more."

"My pleasure, Lawrence," Father Matt replied. "Next, we'll explore the altar and the sanctuary. Each step we take will reveal more about the rich traditions of the Catholic faith."

With a new sense of curiosity, Lawrence followed Father Matt further into the church, ready to uncover the deeper meanings behind these ancient traditions.

The Altar and the Sanctuary

As Lawrence and Father Matt moved deeper into the church, the atmosphere changed subtly. The faint scent of incense still lingering in the air, mingling with the soft, flickering glow of candles. Lawrence couldn't help but feel a sense of awe, despite his skepticism.

"Here we are," Father Matt said, gesturing toward the altar and the sanctuary. "This is the heart of the Catholic Church."

Lawrence took in the scene. The altar was adorned with a white cloth, candles, and a golden crucifix. Behind it, the sanctuary area was slightly elevated, emphasizing its importance.

"So, what's the significance of the altar?" Lawrence asked.

"The altar is the central point of a Catholic church," Father Matt explained. "It's where the Eucharist, also known as the Holy Communion, is celebrated. The altar represents both the table of the Last Supper and the sacrifice of Jesus on the cross."

"That's quite symbolic," Lawrence admitted. "But where does this practice come from?"

"Let's tie it back to Scripture," Father Matt said. "In the Old Testament, the altar was where sacrifices were made to God, as seen in the tabernacle and later in the Temple of Jerusalem. These sacrifices were a way to atone for sins and seek God's favor."

Lawrence nodded, recalling his Bible studies. "Yes, I remember reading about those sacrifices."

"In the New Testament, Jesus fulfills these sacrificial practices," Father Matt continued. 'He is the Lamb of God who takes away the sins of the world', as John the Baptist declares in John 1:29. During the Last

Supper, Jesus established a new covenant, instructing his disciples to 'do this in memory of me' (Luke 22:19). The celebration of the Eucharist is a continuation of that command."

Lawrence's eyes widened. "So, the Mass is a fulfillment of the Last Supper and the sacrifices of the Old Testament?"

"Exactly," Father Matt said with a smile. "The Eucharist is both a sacrifice and a meal, recalling Jesus's sacrifice on the cross and his resurrection. It's a profound mystery where Catholics believe that the bread and wine become the Body and Blood of Christ."

Lawrence took a deep breath, trying to absorb this information. "I've heard of this idea of transubstantiation—the bread and wine becoming the actual body and blood of Christ— but it is a bit hard to grasp."

"It's a mystery of faith," Father Matt acknowledged. "But it's rooted in Jesus's own words at the Last Supper. He said, 'This is my body' and 'This is my blood' (Mark 14:22-24). For Catholics, this isn't just symbolic language; it's a profound reality."

As they continued their tour, Lawrence noticed a golden box behind the altar. "What's that?"

"That's the tabernacle," Father Matt explained. "It's where the consecrated hosts—the Body of Christ—are kept after the Mass. It's a place of reverence and prayer."

Lawrence frowned slightly. "Is there any biblical basis for this?"

"In the Old Testament, the Ark of the Covenant held the presence of God among the Israelites," Father Matt said. "The tabernacle serves a similar purpose. It's a sacred space where Catholics believe Jesus is truly present. This is why you'll often see people genuflect (kneel briefly on one knee) or bow when they pass by."

As they walked through the sanctuary, the soft strains of organ music played in the background, adding to the sacred atmosphere. Lawrence couldn't deny the sense of reverence that permeated the space.

"Tell me about the music," Lawrence said. "It's quite moving."

"Music is an integral part of Catholic worship," Father Matt explained. "It enhances the liturgy and helps lift our hearts and minds to God. This tradition also has biblical roots. In the Old Testament, King David composed psalms and organized musicians to play in the Temple (1 Chronicles 15:16)."

Lawrence nodded thoughtfully. "I can see how that would create a deeper sense of worship."

Father Matt smiled. "Every element you see, hear, and even smell here is designed to draw us closer to God and to help us experience the sacred mysteries of our faith."

As they concluded their exploration of the altar and sanctuary, Lawrence felt a newfound respect for the Catholic traditions he had once viewed with suspicion. He realized there was a depth and richness here that connected the Old and New Testaments in ways he hadn't previously understood.

"Thank you, Father Matt," Lawrence said sincerely. "I'm starting to see things in a new light."

"I'm glad to hear that, Lawrence," Father Matt replied warmly. "Next, we'll explore the significance of statues and icons. Each piece of art tells a story of faith and devotion."

With a new sense of curiosity and openness, Lawrence followed Father Matt, eager to continue his journey of discovery. But before Lawrence and Father Matt continued their exploration, Father Matt showed Lawrence a small cavity in the altar as he pointed to it. "Can you imagine what that cover is for?"

"That," Father Matt said with a knowing smile, "is where we keep a relic of a saint. Every Roman Catholic altar has a relic embedded in it. This tradition dates back to the early Church."

"A relic? Like a piece of a saint's body or something?" Lawrence asked, eyebrows raised.

"Yes, it could be a bone fragment, a piece of clothing, or something the saint touched," Father Matt explained. "It might sound strange at first, but let me explain its significance. The practice is rooted in the respect and honor we give to the Communion of Saints."

"Communion of Saints?" Lawrence echoed.

"The Communion of Saints is the spiritual union of all believers, living and dead, who are part of the body of Christ," Father Matt said. "In the Book of Revelation, John describes the saints in heaven interceding for us (Revelation 5:8). Having relics in our altars reminds us that when we celebrate the Mass, we are united with the entire Church—those on earth and those in heaven."

"So, it's like a way to feel connected to the history and community of the Church?" Lawrence asked.

"Exactly," Father Matt replied. "It's a tangible reminder that we are part of a larger spiritual family. The relics also remind us of the holiness we are all called to and the examples set by the saints who came before us."

Lawrence nodded slowly, beginning to appreciate the depth of these traditions. "I see. It's not just about the object itself, but what it represents."

"Precisely," Father Matt said. "And speaking of representations, let's move on to the statues and icons. Each one has its own story and significance, like this picture of St Peter. We know the artist who painted this picture intended people to know that it was Saint Peter, because he holds in his hand the keys to the kingdom, given to him by Christ in Matthew 16:13–20. The other hand, his right, has the first three fingers up, depicting that he believed and taught about the Trinity – the Father, the Son and the Holy Spirit. Pictures of Jesus often have those three fingers up".

Statues and Icons

As they walked towards the side aisles of the church, Lawrence noticed various statues and icons placed in niches and on pedestals. The stained-glass windows depicted vivid scenes of saints and biblical events.

"Statues and icons are something I've always found puzzling," Lawrence admitted. "Why do Catholics have so many images of saints?"

"Again, statues and icons serve as visual reminders of the saints and their exemplary lives of faith," Father Matt explained. "They inspire us to follow their examples and remind us of the virtues they embodied. It's important to understand that Catholics do not worship these images; we venerate them. There's a significant difference."

Lawrence looked closely at a statue of St. Francis of Assisi. "Venerate? Can you explain that?"

"Of course," Father Matt said. "To venerate means to honor or respect. When we venerate saints, we acknowledge their holiness and ask for their intercession before God. This practice has biblical roots. In the Old Testament, God commanded the use of images, such as the cherubim on the Ark of the Covenant (Exodus 25:18-20). These images served to remind the Israelites of God's presence."

"But isn't that against the commandment about graven images?" Lawrence asked.

"God's commandment against graven images was against the worship of idols—false gods," Father Matt clarified. "The images and statues in the Catholic Church are not idols. They are visual aids that lift our hearts and minds to God, much like the pictures of loved ones we keep in our homes remind us of our connection to them."

As they walked past a stained-glass window depicting St. Peter, Lawrence marveled at the vibrant colors and intricate designs. "These windows are beautiful. What's their purpose?"

"Stained glass windows serve several purposes," Father Matt said. "Historically, they were used to educate the faithful, especially when many people were illiterate. The windows tell stories from the Bible and the lives of the saints, making these stories accessible to everyone. They also add beauty to the church, creating an environment that lifts the spirit and inspires worship."

Lawrence gazed at the window, now seeing it in a new light. "So, everything here has a purpose, a deeper meaning."

"Yes," Father Matt affirmed. "Every element you see, hear, and even smell in the church is designed to draw us closer to God and to help us experience the sacred mysteries of our faith."

As they moved to another part of the church, Lawrence felt a growing respect for the rich traditions and deep symbolism within the Catholic faith. He realized there was much more to explore and understand.

"Thank you, Father Matt," Lawrence said sincerely. "I'm beginning to see the beauty and depth in these practices."

"I'm glad to hear that, Lawrence," Father Matt replied warmly. "Next, let's take a look at the Stations of the Cross. They're a powerful way to meditate on the Passion of Christ."

With a renewed sense of curiosity and openness, Lawrence followed Father Matt, eager to continue his journey of discovery.

The Stations of the Cross

As Lawrence and Father Matt continued their tour, they stopped in front of a series of small images arranged along the walls of the church. Each depicted a different scene from the final hours of Jesus's life.

"These are the Stations of the Cross," Father Matt explained. "They represent 14 key events from Jesus's journey to Calvary. Walking and praying through these stations are a way to meditate on Christ's Passion and sacrifice for us."

Lawrence studied the images closely. "So, it's like a spiritual pilgrimage?"

"Exactly," Father Matt replied. "Catholics often pray the Stations of the Cross, especially during Lent, to deepen their connection with Jesus's suffering and to reflect on His love for us."

Lawrence nodded, seeing the reverence with which Father Matt spoke. "It's a powerful way to remember what Jesus went through."

"Yes," Father Matt agreed. "And it helps us unite our own sufferings with His, finding strength and hope in His sacrifice."

Votive Candles and Prayer Cards

Moving to another area of the church, Father Matt and Lawrence came upon a side altar adorned with flickering candles. Nearby, a table held prayer cards and rosary beads.

"These are votive candles," Father Matt said. "Lighting a candle is a way to symbolize our prayers rising to God. It's a physical act that represents our intention to keep our prayers alive even after we've left the church."

Lawrence watched as someone lit a candle, knelt, and offered a silent prayer. "So, it's not just about the candle, but what it signifies?"

"Exactly," Father Matt said. "It's a way to express our prayers visually and spiritually. The light of the candle symbolizes Christ as the Light of the World, and our prayers joining His light."

Lawrence picked up a prayer card. "And these?"

"Prayer cards usually have images of saints, along with prayers asking for their intercession," Father Matt explained. "Catholics believe in the Communion of Saints, where saints in heaven pray for us, just as we ask our friends on earth to pray for us and our sick family and friends."

"Why ask saints to pray for us?" Lawrence asked, genuinely curious.

"Because they are close to God, having lived lives of exemplary holiness," Father Matt said. "They intercede for us, adding their prayers to ours. It's a powerful reminder that we're part of a larger spiritual family."

Father Matt then picked up a set of rosary beads. "And these are rosary beads. The rosary is a form of prayer that meditates on the key events in the lives of Jesus and Mary. Each bead represents a prayer, and as we pray, we reflect on these events."

Lawrence held the rosary, feeling its weight. "It's a way to keep focus in prayer, isn't it?"

"Yes, it helps us stay focused and meditate deeply," Father Matt confirmed. "And by reflecting on the mysteries of the rosary, we're drawn into the life of Christ and His mother."

Even many Catholics think it's about the "Our Fathers" and the "Hail Marys" which are the reason for the Rosary – but it's so much more about giving people something they might like to do, what they can do without a lot of brain power, but really meditating on the mystery of the Rosary itself. There are four sets of Mysteries - Joyful, Sorrowful, Glorious and the Luminous Mysteries, representing various times in Jesus and His Mother Mary's life, a mixture of bad and good. Each mystery has five themes we call decades. For example, the five decades of the Joyful Mystery are "The Annunciation" - *Luke 1:26-27*; "The Visitation" - *Luke 1:39-42*; "The Nativity" - *Luke 2:1-7*; "The Presentation in the Temple" - *Luke 2:21-24*; and "The Finding in the Temple" - *Luke 2:41-47*.

Father Matt continued, "Lawrence, remember at the stained windows I told you that they help teach stories to those who couldn't read or write? The same this is true with the Rosary. But with the Rosary, the Church Fathers selected initially three important Mysteries, and along with them the top 5 biblical themes, so as people worked out in the fields, or bringing crops to the market, they could easily pray the Rosary and keep these biblical stories alive in their daily activities."

Lawrence asked, "So it never was about praying to Mary?" Father Matt replied, "Well, Mary is the Mother of God. So it is important to be respectful and ask Her for Her intercession, just like the servants told Mary that there was no more wine at the wedding feast in Cana. Jesus said that His time had not come yet. But Mary desired that His ministry start that day. So She asked Him. He deeply respected His Mom and did as She asked. Why would She not do the same for a request of ours?"

Lawrence persisted in his questioning about Mary, "why would someone have to say fifty Hail Mary's in the Rosary?" Father chuckled a bit and said "Let's look at it this way. Most of us take great pride in our ability to multitask. With the Rosary, saying ten Hail Marys ensures that you are spending adequate time in this multitasking activity to fully meditate on that particular mystery. Think of the 10 Hail Mary's as a prayerful place holder." Lawrence agreed that this makes sense.

The Path to Sainthood

As they continued their tour, Father Matt led Lawrence to a quiet corner of the church. "Now, let's talk about sainthood and the canonization process," he said. "Becoming a saint sounds like a long, complex process" Lawrence noted.

"It is" Father Matt agreed. "The Church takes it very seriously. To be canonized as a saint, a person must live a life of heroic virtue and be credited with participation of miracles after their death."

"Miracles?" Lawrence asked, intrigued.

"Yes," Father Matt said. "When people pray to a deceased person asking for their intercession, and God grants a miracle through those prayers, it's seen as a sign of the person's holiness." "And the Church verifies these miracles?" Lawrence inquired.

"Indeed," Father Matt said. "There's a rigorous process involving medical experts, theologians, and the Congregation for the Causes of Saints. The process can take many years. First, the person is declared 'Venerable' if they lived a life of heroic virtue. Then, after one miracle, they're beatified and called 'Blessed.' After a second verified miracle, they are canonized as a saint."

Lawrence looked thoughtful. "So, the Church is very careful about this." "Absolutely," Father Matt confirmed. "It's a thorough and deliberate process to ensure that those declared saints truly lived lives of exemplary holiness and are worthy of veneration."

Participating in the Mass

Father Matt and Lawrence sat down in a pew near the back of the church. The quiet, reverent atmosphere was punctuated by the soft murmur of a few parishioners praying.

"Lawrence," Father Matt began, "I'd like to invite you to attend and participate in a Catholic Mass. It's the central act of Catholic worship and a beautiful way to experience our faith."

Lawrence shifted slightly. "I'd be open to that, but I'm not Catholic. How can I participate?"

Father Matt smiled reassuringly. "You can join us in the prayers and hymns, and during the Communion line, you can come forward for a blessing instead of receiving the Eucharist. Just cross your arms over your chest to indicate you're not receiving Communion, and the priest will give you a blessing."

"What about the different parts of the Mass?" Lawrence asked.

"The Mass has two main parts: the Liturgy of the Word and the Liturgy of the Eucharist," Father Matt explained. "The Liturgy of the Word includes three readings from the Bible, a homily, and prayers of the faithful. The Liturgy of the Eucharist involves the consecration of the bread and wine and the distribution of Communion."

"And what's the significance of each part?" Lawrence inquired.

"The Liturgy of the Word focuses on hearing and reflecting on God's Word," Father Matt said. "The Liturgy of the Eucharist is a re-presentation of the Last Supper and Jesus's sacrifice on the cross. It's where Catholics believe the bread and wine become the Body and Blood of Christ."

Lawrence nodded, absorbing this information. "It sounds like a profound experience."

"It is," Father Matt agreed. "And if you ever feel called to become a part of the Catholic Church, there are steps you can take. You'd go through a process called the Rite of Christian Initiation for Adults (RCIA), which includes instruction in the faith, spiritual formation, and the reception of the sacraments."

"What kind of steps are involved?" Lawrence asked.

"RCIA typically involves several months of classes and spiritual guidance," Father Matt explained. "You'd learn about the Catholic faith, its teachings, and its practices. At the end of this period, you'd be received into the Church, usually at the Easter Vigil, and receive the sacraments of Baptism (if not already baptized), Confirmation, and Eucharist."

Lawrence smiled. "Thank you, Father Matt. This has been incredibly enlightening. I've learned so much already, and I'm looking forward to attending a Mass and see where that leads me."

"I'm glad to hear that, Lawrence," Father Matt said warmly. "Remember, you're always welcome here, whether you're just exploring or feel called to join us more fully. Faith is a journey, and we're here to walk with you every step of the way."

The Call

It was Saturday evening, about 9 pm and the rectory phone rang. "St. Michael's, this is Father Matt. How can I help you?" It was Lawrence. He said "Father, I wanted to thank you for taking the time to show me around Saint Michael's Church and explaining what I am starting to realize is the richness of Catholic Doctrine". This really wet my appetite to know more. I'd really like to observe a Catholic Mass. What are the times tomorrow?" Father Matt responded, "Lawrence, I have been praying that you ever since our impromptu appointment on Tuesday. I, myself explored a few different denominational services prior to entering the seminary. Our services tomorrow start at 7 am, 9:30 am and 11 am. I know you have an hour drive to get here, so the later Masses might fit your schedule better."

Lawrence responded, "Thank you Father. Someday, it would be great to hear your comments about your experiences at other church services. I think I would like to attend the 11 am Mass. I will be able to attend my normal service at 8 am and make it in time for that Mass. Is there any chance we could chat after Mass? I plan to take notes on what I see and what my questions are."

Father Matt said, "That would be great! We could go over to the rectory and fix a sandwich and grab a cup of coffee and chat". Lawrence said "That would be great! What can I bring?"

Father Matt responded, "Not a thing, other than your notepad. I will see if James can join us. Did I tell you that he has been studying to become a Deacon? He might have some good answers for your questions as well." Lawrence said, "That would be awesome! I would like to extend my thanks once again. My car is working great!"

The Mass

As Lawrence found a spot to sit in one of the pews one or two back from the front pew, he looked around at the people coming in for the 11 o'clock Mass at St. Michael's Church. His mind immediately began to recall and compare the surroundings, the sounds and level of excitement with the church service he had just attended at his own home Evangelical Church.

He recalled how as the sun rose, its first light spilled into the church through large, clear windows, casting a bright and inviting glow over the modern sanctuary. The atmosphere was charged with a palpable sense of excitement and anticipation, a buzz of energy that permeates the space, very different from what he sensed he would experience in the hour or so to come.

The sanctuary back home itself is designed to be welcoming and comfortable, with rows of cushioned chairs arranged in a semicircle around the stage. The stage is adorned with vibrant backdrops and colorful lighting, creating a dynamic and engaging environment. The scent of freshly brewed coffee wafts from the lobby, where congregants are greeted with warm smiles and friendly handshakes.

In contrast at this Catholic Church, as the congregation filed in, they immediately went over to the Holy Water and blessed themselves and the greeters stood there smiling with their hands clasped facing the door everyone was entering. The greeters would smile and nod, and maybe say hello or good morning. There were no refreshments and the church-goers moved rapidly into the worship space and to a pew.

Lawrence thought they all must sit in the same spot every week because they only seemed to be friendly to those immediately around them.

Usually in Lawrence's church, as people find their seats, the worship band would be on stages and beginning to tune their instruments. The hum of electric guitars, the thump of the bass, and the crisp beat of the drums create an anticipatory rhythm. The lead vocalist would occasionally step up to the microphone and offers a cheerful "Good morning, everyone!" which is met with enthusiastic responses and applause from the congregation.

The service at Lawrence's church officially begins with an upbeat worship song. The band launches into a lively and spirited performance, their music filling the room with a joyful and contagious energy. The congregation stands, claps, and sings along, their voices merging with the music in a powerful expression of collective worship. The lyrics, projected onto large screens, encourage participation and create a sense of unity and shared purpose.

It was very different here at Saint Michael's. The music was all from the back of the church, in the choir loft, where the choir was gathering and the organist was organizing her music sheets. Noone was on the altar other than the altar servers who were busy trying to light the candles. Many people there, including myself wanted to tell the one altar server that the tall candle was lit, even though he backed up several times, he still couldn't tell it was lit!

Back at my church, at this point before the service began, the Children would be heading toward their designated areas for Sunday school, their excited chatter adding to the lively atmosphere. Volunteers, wearing bright, identifiable T-shirts, guide them with friendly smiles and reassuring words.

Here, the kids stayed with their family. Some people wore jeans and a shirt, while others wore suit and tie and dress shoes and some of the women wore longer style dresses and some of the women wore some type of scarf on their head. Lawrence thought to take notes on all of that, especially the head covering.

He thought of when he first saw his own pastor early in the morning, dressed casually in jeans and a button-down shirt, as he stepped onto the stage. He exudes warmth and approachability, his presence commanding attention without a hint of formality. With a wide smile, he greets the congregation. "Welcome to our Sunday service! We're so glad you're here with us today. Let's open in prayer."

Lawrence remembered his pastor leading the opening prayer, and how the room quieted slightly, but the sense of community remains strong. Heads bowed, and a serene stillness descended, punctuated only by the occasional murmur of agreement and soft "Amens" from the crowd.

After the prayer, his pastor shares a few announcements, highlighting upcoming events and opportunities for involvement within the church community. His tone was engaging and conversational, making everyone feel included and valued.

Lawrence remembered as the service transitioned back to worship, the lights dim slightly, and the band resumes with a mix of contemporary worship songs and heartfelt ballads. The congregation was invited to reflect, to lift their hands in praise, or to simply stand and soak in the presence of the moment.

In these initial moments, Lawrence thought his church's evangelical service struck a good balance between celebration and reflection, fostering an environment that is both uplifting and deeply spiritual. In that beginning of their Sunday gathering, it was a time to connect with God and one another, to celebrate faith, and to draw strength from the communal experience.

LAWRENCE'S MIND QUICKLY returned in thought, sight and presence to the 11 o'clock Mass. He had his notebook and followed along in the missalette. When everyone else sat, he sat. When they stood, he stood. When they knelt, he knelt. He had decided the only way he could determine the value is to be as immersed in the service as he was able to, remembering that Father Matt told him to cross his hands when he was moving up the Communion line.

Even though he loved his own church's contemporary Christian music, he was quite impressed with the choir, the scripture readings and the reverence the congregation had during the Eucharistic portion of the Mass. But the more he saw, the more notes he took and questions he had for Father Matt. He was happy to see that James was there as an adult Altar Server and hoped that James could join he and Father for a sandwich after the Mass ended.

After the Mass concluded, Father Matt and James returned to the front of the church to the pew where Lawrence was sitting, compiling his notes. Lawrence jumped to his feet and warmly embraced Father Matt and James with a warm handshake and special thanks to James for his help fixing his car earlier in the week.

The three walked together to the rectory's kitchen and started making sandwiches and pouring themselves a cup of coffee. Father Matt watched as Lawrence flipped through the pages of notes and questions and said, "James, you better grab your bible and the Catechism, we might need that to reference as we get stumped by some of Lawrence's questions.

Introductory rites:
Sign of the Cross

Lawrence said, "first, help me understand what the Sign of the Cross entails. When Catholics make the Sign of the Cross, they touch their forehead, chest, and both shoulders, while saying, 'In the name of the Father, and of the Son, and of the Holy Spirit. Amen.' This simple yet powerful act is a way of professing faith in the Holy Trinity and invoking the three Persons of God's blessing. Is that right?"

James said, "Father, eat your sandwich. We just covered the Biblical Roots and Symbolism of the Sign of the Cross in my Deaconate class. Let me try and answer this"

In Ezekiel 9:4-6, there's an early foreshadowing of a sign that marks God's people. The prophet sees a vision where the faithful are marked on their foreheads to be spared from judgment. This imagery parallels the Sign of the Cross, marking believers as belonging to God and under His protection.

In Ezekiel 1:3, we see the importance of the Lord's hand upon Ezekiel, symbolizing divine calling and empowerment. Making the Sign of the Cross reminds us that God's hand is upon us, guiding and strengthening us in our daily lives.

Psalm 54:1 cries out, "Save me, O God, by your name; vindicate me by your might." When we make the Sign of the Cross, we are invoking God's name, acknowledging our need for His salvation and help. It's a prayer for deliverance, echoing the psalmist's plea for rescue.

Paul proclaims that God exalted Jesus and gave Him the name above every name, so that at the name of Jesus every knee should bow in Philippians 2:9-11. The Sign of the Cross is a tangible way to honor the name of Jesus, reminding us of His supreme authority and power in even uttering His Holy Name and our showing Him, anywhere, public or private that worship and love Him.

Matthew 18:20 assures us, "For where two or three gather in my name, there am I with them." When we gather and make the Sign of the Cross, it reinforces Christ's presence among us, a comforting reminder that He is with us in our communal and personal prayers.

Finally, in John 14:13, Jesus promises, "And I will do whatever you ask in my name, so that the Father may be glorified in the Son." The Sign of the Cross, made in the name of the Father, Son, and Holy Spirit, is a prayerful action that brings our petitions before God, aligning our prayers with His will.

Father Matt added "The Sign of the Cross is more than a mere ritual; it is a profound expression of faith, a summary of the Scriptures, and a declaration of God's triune nature. It connects us to the early Christians, marks us as God's own, invokes His protection and blessings, and brings us into the presence of Christ."

Lawrence answered "As an evangelical Christian, I see it as a physical manifestation of the prayerful heart, a way to live out Paul's command to "pray without ceasing" (1 Thessalonians 5:17). Every time I make this sign, I are reminded of God's love, Christ's sacrifice, and the Holy Spirit's guidance. It's a small act with deep roots in Scripture and rich with meaning, uniting us all with Christians across the ages."

The Lord Be With You

Lawrence said "Next thing I wrote down was 'The Lord be with you' and the response of the congregation was 'And with your Spirit'. What was that exchange all about?"

Father Matt said I'll take that one, and half-jokingly grabbed the bible from James, "The phrase 'The Lord be with you' and the response 'And with your spirit' is a beautiful exchange that takes place during the introductory rites of the Catholic Mass. Let's explore its depth and significance by grounding it in Scripture and connecting it to our faith."

He continued, "In Exodus 3:10-12, When God calls Moses to lead the Israelites out of Egypt, Moses is understandably apprehensive. God reassures him by saying, 'I will be with you.' This promise of God's presence was a source of strength and courage for Moses. Similarly, when the priest says, 'The Lord be with you,' he is invoking God's reassuring presence upon the congregation, reminding them that God is with them in their journey of faith."

"Further, in Judges 6:14-18: Gideon, like Moses, feels inadequate for the task God assigns to him. When the angel of the Lord appears to Gideon and tells him to save Israel from the Midianites, Gideon expresses his doubts. The angel reassures him with, 'The Lord is with you, mighty warrior.' This assurance of God's presence empowers Gideon. In the Mass, the priest's greeting, 'The Lord be with you', similarly empowers the faithful, acknowledging that God's presence equips them for their spiritual battles and daily lives."

Father said, "another great reference is Numbers 13:32-33, when the Israelite spies return from exploring the Promised Land, they report feeling like 'grasshoppers' compared to the inhabitants. Their fear stems from forgetting God's promise to be with them. The greeting 'The Lord be with you' serves as a reminder of God's continual presence and support, countering any feelings of inadequacy or fear among the congregation."

"... and my personal favorite is Joshua 1:4-6 and 9, As Joshua takes up the mantle of leadership after Moses, God repeatedly assures him, 'I will be with you; I will never leave you nor forsake you.' This divine presence is the foundation of Joshua's courage and success. The greeting 'The Lord be with you' at Mass echoes this assurance, reminding the congregation that God's steadfast presence is with them, giving them courage and hope.

James chimed in about the response "And with your spirit", "It has its roots in Paul's epistles. In several of his letters, Paul uses a similar phrase to bless and encourage his readers in 2 Timothy 4:22 and Galatians 6:18, when the congregation responds this way, they are acknowledging the unique role of the priest, who, through his ordination, has received the Holy Spirit in a special way to lead the community in worship."

Father said "in Matthew 28:20, Jesus' final words to His disciples are, 'And surely I am with you always, to the very end of the age.' This promise of Christ's abiding presence is the heart of the priest's greeting. When the priest says, 'The Lord be with you,' he is echoing Jesus' promise, reminding the faithful that Christ is always with them."

Fathe Matt continued, "Jesus speaks of the Holy Spirit as the Advocate who will be with His followers forever in John 14:16-17. This divine presence of the Holy Spirit is invoked during the Mass. The greeting and response reflect this profound truth: the Holy Spirit dwells within us, guiding, comforting, and strengthening us."

James added "The exchange 'The Lord be with you' and 'And with your spirit' is not just a ritualistic formality but a profound personal and communal affirmation of faith. It serves as a mutual blessing between the priest and the congregation. The priest prays that God's presence be with the people, and the people pray that God's Spirit be with the priest, especially as he leads them in worship."

"For you, as an evangelical Christian, this exchange might resonate with the deep sense of community and mutual encouragement that is so central to our faith. It is a moment of unity, where we recognize God's presence among us and within each of us, enabling us to worship Him more fully", James so eloquently said.

Father Matt continued, "In summary, this beautiful liturgical greeting and response encapsulate the core of our faith: God's abiding presence with His people. It draws from the rich scriptural tradition of God's promises and reassurances, serving as a powerful reminder of His constant companionship and the empowerment of the Holy Spirit in our lives."

Confiteor

Lawrence seemed very perplexed and appeared afraid to ask this question, "Father, the next thing I wrote down was about what seemed like a communal confession. I thought you said that the Confessional was where people go to confess their sins and receive absolution. Can you help me understand this part of the Mass?"

Father replied, "Lawrence, I'm so glad you're curious about the Catholic Mass, particularly the prayer that begins with 'I confess.' This prayer, called the Confiteor, is a beautiful expression of humility and repentance, drawing us closer to God's mercy and grace. Let's explore its depth by looking at some key scriptural passages and then talk about sin and the types of sin as we go."

Father Matt continued "'In Psalm 32:5, the psalmist declares, 'Then I acknowledged my sin to you and did not cover up my iniquity. I said, 'I will confess my transgressions to the Lord.' And you forgave the guilt of my sin.' This verse encapsulates the heart of the Confiteor, where we openly acknowledge our sins before God and seek His forgiveness. It reminds us that confession leads to the experience of God's mercy."

Father continued, "John writes in 1 John 1:9, 'If we confess our sins, He is faithful and just and will forgive us our sins and purify us from all unrighteousness.' This promise assures us that our confession is met with God's faithfulness and forgiveness. The Confiteor echoes this assurance, reaffirming our trust in God's just and purifying love."

James said, "In James 5:16 James encourages believers to 'confess your sins to each other and pray for each other so that you may be healed.' This verse highlights the communal aspect of confession. In the

Confiteor, we confess our sinful nature not just individually but also as a community, recognizing that our sins affect the whole Body of Christ. This collective confession fosters unity and mutual support, while we know as part of our formal sacramental preparation and informal training that mortal sins require personal confession, typically in the confessional in the church."

Father Matt chimes in again saying "James makes a good point about our sinful nature. Since Adam and Eve, we have been cursed with a predisposition to sinful ways. This doesn't mean we should throw our arms in the air and give into sin. In the parable of the Pharisee and the tax collector in Luke 18:13-14, the tax collector stands at a distance, beats his breast, and says, 'God, have mercy on me, a sinner.' Jesus tells us that this man went home justified before God. The Confiteor reflects this attitude of humility and contrition. When we say, 'through my fault, through my fault, through my most grievous fault,' we are adopting the tax collector's posture, acknowledging our deep need for God's mercy. This atones for the small sins we refer to as 'venial' sins."

James reminded us in Hebrews 12:1, "This verse speaks of being 'surrounded by such a great cloud of witnesses', referring to the saints who have gone before us. In the Confiteor, we ask for the intercession of 'Blessed Mary ever-Virgin, all the angels and saints, and you, my brothers and sisters.' This reminds us that we are part of a larger spiritual family, supported by the prayers of the saints and our fellow believers."

Father concluded this part of the discussion with "In Psalm 51:10, David had a heartfelt plea, 'Create in me a pure heart, O God, and renew a steadfast spirit within me'. That aligns with the purpose of the Confiteor. By confessing our sins at the beginning of Mass, we are asking God to purify our hearts and prepare us to fully participate in the sacred mysteries of the Eucharist."

Father continues, "The Confiteor is a profound prayer that encapsulates the essence of repentance, communal solidarity, and reliance on God's infinite mercy. By acknowledging our sins and seeking forgiveness, we open our hearts to receive God's grace more fully."

Lawrence replied, "this explanation helps me see the beauty and depth of the Confiteor. It's a moment of great humility and grace, setting the tone for the entire Mass, as we prepare ourselves to encounter the living God in the liturgy."

Lord Have Mercy

James said "Lawrence, Father Matt and I, along with our Catholic men's group have been praying for you to be filled with the Holy Spirit, but I have never witnessed such an immediate and obvious answer to our prayer!"

Lawrence responded "Thanks for noticing this in me, but to be honest, I am nervous. This is all so new to me and I have so many questions left. Like why is the Confiteor immediately followed up with a prayer starting with 'Lord have Mercy'... isn't that redundant? What do you think Father Matt?"

Father replied "Of course, Lawrence! I understand why it might seem redundant at first glance, but let me explain why these prayers, though similar in theme, are distinct and complementary in their purpose."

"The Confiteor is a comprehensive acknowledgment of our sins. We confess our faults, express our sorrow, and take responsibility for our actions. This prayer is about laying our hearts bare before God and the community, admitting that we have failed in our thoughts, words, deeds, and omissions."

He continued, "The prayer that follows, the "Lord, have mercy" (or Kyrie, eleison in Greek), is a petition that goes beyond mere acknowledgment of sin. It is a heartfelt cry for divine mercy. While the Confiteor is our confession, the Kyrie is our plea for God's compassion and healing."

James broke into the conversation to add "In Scripture, we see a pattern where confession is often followed by a plea for mercy. Consider

Psalm 51, David's great prayer of repentance. After confessing his sin, David repeatedly asks for God's mercy and cleansing: 'Have mercy on me, O God, according to your unfailing love; according to your great compassion blot out my transgressions' (Psalm 51:1)."

Father added, "Similarly, in Luke 18:13, the tax collector's prayer is twofold. He first acknowledges his sinfulness by saying, 'God, have mercy on me, a sinner.' This shows how confession and a plea for mercy are intertwined, forming a complete act of repentance and dependence on God's grace."

"By following the Confiteor with 'Lord, have mercy,' we emphasize our utter dependence on God's mercy. It reminds us that forgiveness is not something we can earn or demand; it is a gift from God. This petition helps to humble us and recognize that without God's grace, we cannot stand righteous before Him." Father concluded.

James added a bit more, "In the liturgy, these prayers also serve to prepare our hearts for what is to come. The Confiteor and the Kyrie set the tone for the remainder of the Mass, leading us from recognition of our sins to a plea for mercy, and finally to the reception of God's word and the Eucharist. This progression helps us spiritually cleanse and open ourselves to God's presence and action in the Mass."

James persisted on, "Repeating the plea for mercy isn't redundancy but rather a deepening of our prayer. Think of it as similar to how we might apologize and then ask for forgiveness in human relationships. The repetition and different expressions underscore the sincerity and depth of our repentance and our trust in the mercy of the one we have wronged."

Father added, "So, Lawrence, these prayers are like different facets of the same gem. They reflect our journey from recognizing our sinfulness to earnestly seeking and receiving God's mercy. Together, they create a fuller, richer expression of our contrition and reliance on God's grace."

Gloria

Lawrence asked if he could have another cup of coffee. "It is so good and compliments the discussion about the Mass. The Gloria was so nice and I look forward to details about that!"

Father said, "Lawrence, you're not going to believe this, but this is 'Mystic Monk Coffee, Cowboy Blend'. We like it because it has notes of cocoa, caramel, vanilla and a hint of aromatic herbs. The good thing is it is great black because of the flavorings or with cream. But you are right, Lawrence. The Gloria is one of my favorites as well. Let's jump into it."

He continued, "The Gloria is a joyful hymn of praise that has a significant place in the Catholic Mass. It's a prayer that lifts our hearts and minds to God, celebrating His glory and majesty. This hymn of praise, known as the Gloria in Excelsis Deo, is an ancient and profound part of our liturgy. It helps us transition from acknowledging our sins to celebrating God's glory and grace. Let's explore its scriptural roots and significance.

"The Gloria begins with the words the angels proclaimed at Jesus' birth: 'Glory to God in the highest, and on earth peace to people of good will' (Luke 2:14). This connects us to the heavenly praise of God and reminds us of the Incarnation, when God became man to bring peace and salvation to humanity."

James found a few appropriate Scriptural Readings "Psalm 29:1-2 says 'Give unto the Lord the glory due to His name; worship the Lord in the beauty of holiness.' The Gloria echoes this psalm, calling us to give glory to God and worship Him with all our hearts. In Psalm 96:2-3, it says 'Sing to the Lord, bless His name; proclaim the good news of

His salvation from day to day. Declare His glory among the nations, His wonders among all peoples.' In the Gloria, we sing of God's glory and proclaim His wonders, fulfilling this scriptural call to worship."

Father went on to say, "The Gloria continues with a series of acclamations about God's nature, 'We praise you, we bless you, we adore you, we glorify you, we give you thanks for your great glory.' This phrase acknowledges God's greatness and our response of worship. Each of these statement draws from various scriptures that speak of God's attributes and our call to praise Him."

"Like Revelation 4:11, 'You are worthy, our Lord and God, to receive glory and honor and power, for you created all things, and by your will they were created and have their being.' The Gloria reflects this heavenly worship, joining our voices with those of the angels and saints." Added James.

He continued, "The Gloria also focuses on Jesus Christ, reflecting on His role in our salvation, 'Lord Jesus Christ, Only Begotten Son, Lord God, Lamb of God, Son of the Father, you take away the sins of the world, have mercy on us; you take away the sins of the world, receive our prayer; you are seated at the right hand of the Father, have mercy on us.' This part of the Gloria draws from several key scriptural passages - John 1:29 'Behold the Lamb of God, who takes away the sin of the world.' Revelation 5:9 says 'You are worthy to take the scroll and to open its seals, because you were slain, and with your blood you purchased for God persons from every tribe and language and people and nation.' And Hebrews 1:3 says 'The Son is the radiance of God's glory and the exact representation of his being, sustaining all things by his powerful word. After he had provided purification for sins, he sat down at the right hand of the Majesty in heaven.'

Father Matt says, "The Gloria concludes with a Trinitarian doxology – 'For you alone are the Holy One, you alone are the Lord, you alone are the Most High, Jesus Christ, with the Holy Spirit, in the glory of God the Father. Amen.' Lawrence, can you find anything in Scripture which reflects this Trinitarian praise and recognizes the unity and majesty of the Father, Son, and Holy Spirit?"

Lawrence opens his bible to a bookmark and responds, "how about Matthew 28:19 which states 'Therefore go and make disciples of all nations, baptizing them in the name of the Father and of the Son and of the Holy Spirit.'? And 2 Corinthians 13:14 which says 'May the grace of the Lord Jesus Christ, and the love of God, and the fellowship of the Holy Spirit be with you all.'"?

Father Matt acknowledged, "Very Good Lawrence! The Gloria is a rich tapestry of scriptural praise, bringing together elements from both the Old and New Testaments. It is a powerful proclamation of God's glory, the redemptive work of Christ, and the unity of the Holy Trinity. By singing the Gloria, we join the angels and saints in their eternal hymn of praise, lifting our hearts to God in joyful adoration."

He continued, "Lawrence, I hope this helps you see the Gloria not as a mere liturgical formality, but as a vibrant, biblical hymn that connects us to the heavenly worship and deepens our experience of God's presence in the Mass. The next part of the Mass, we will transition to what we call 'The Liturgy of the Word'. I am sure that you can guess why it's called that."

The Liturgy of the Word

Lawrence then says "yes, Father Matt, I love the scriptures, especially the New Testament. As an evangelical, I can quote these scriptures forward and backward. My parents and pastors over the years have convinced me that God is the Author of Scripture, and we need to rely on the power of Scripture in our lives. I really didn't know that Catholics read Scripture in your services or otherwise! But why were there readings from the Old Testament, the New Testament, Gospel and in between there was an interactive reading of one of David's Psalms. Why that format?"

Father Matt replied "You're not alone Lawrence! I think a lot of non-Catholic people don't realize everything we do is based on Scripture! Your own love for Scripture is wonderful and it's something we deeply cherish in the Catholic faith as well. The structure of the readings during Mass is very intentional and deeply rooted in both tradition and Scripture itself. Let's explore why the Mass includes readings from the Old Testament, the Psalms, and the New Testament."

James spoke up, "The Bible is indeed the living word of God and central to our worship. The format of our readings during Mass has deep biblical and theological significance. Let's walk through the reasons for this structure"

"We believe that all of Scripture, both Old and New Testaments, is the inspired word of God and that the Old Testament prefigures and prepares for the New, while the New Testament fulfills and completes the Old. By including readings from both Testaments, we see the unity and continuity of God's salvation plan throughout history."

Father Matt opened the bible to Romans 15:4 and says, "Paul writes, 'For everything that was written in the past was written to teach us, so that through the endurance taught in the Scriptures and the encouragement they provide we might have hope.' The Old Testament readings help us understand the foundations of our faith and see God's faithfulness to His promises."

Then he continued "in Luke 24:27 it says how after His resurrection, Jesus explains to the disciples on the road to Emmaus how all the Scriptures point to Him – 'And beginning with Moses and all the Prophets, he explained to them what was said in all the Scriptures concerning himself.' Reading from the Old Testament allows us to see Christ prefigured and foreshadowed in the events, prophecies, and writings of the Hebrew Scriptures. When we get to the Eucharist, we will show you it's Jewish Roots, which is not surprising - Jesus, Mary, Joseph, anyone who could have influenced Him was either Jewish or hated Jews because of what they believed. I guess much of that has not changed, unfortunately!"

James took over, saying, "The Psalms are a vital part of our worship because they are the prayers and songs inspired by the Holy Spirit. They express a range of human emotions and experiences, allowing us to connect deeply with God through praise, lament, thanksgiving, and supplication. Putting them between the first and second reading can be a welcome buffer."

"St. Paul in Ephesians 5:19, encourages the early Christians to 'speak to one another with psalms, hymns, and songs from the Spirit. Sing and make music from your heart to the Lord.' The responsorial nature of the Psalm—where the congregation responds with a refrain—makes it a communal prayer, engaging the whole assembly in the worship in what is generally pretty uplifting." James continued.

Father explained, "The New Testament readings, often from the Epistles, provide teachings and exhortations for living out our Christian faith. They show us how the early Church understood and applied the teachings of Jesus. For instance in 2 Timothy 3:16-17, Paul reminds us, 'All Scripture is God-breathed and is useful for teaching, rebuking, correcting and training in righteousness, so that the servant of God may be thoroughly equipped for every good work.' These readings help equip us for our journey of faith."

James interjects, "The Gospel reading holds a place of special prominence because it contains the words and deeds of Jesus Christ, our Savior. During the Gospel reading, we stand in reverence to acknowledge the centrality of Jesus in our faith. In John 6:68, Peter says to Jesus, 'Lord, to whom shall we go? You have the words of eternal life.' The Gospels are the heart of the Scriptures because they tell us directly about Jesus' life, teachings, death, and resurrection."

Father Matt sips his coffee and explains, "This sequence of readings—Old Testament, which sometimes we use a New Testament Epistle in place of the Old Testament as the First Reading, the a reading from the Psalms, a New Testament reading, and then the Gospel—reflects the rhythm of God's revelation and our response. It takes us on a journey through salvation history, deepening our understanding and drawing us into the mystery of Christ."

Continuing, Father says "In Nehemiah 8:1-3 and 8, we see an example of the liturgical reading of Scripture. The Israelites gathered to hear the reading of the Law, and the Levites helped the people to understand it. This practice of reading and interpreting Scripture in a communal setting has ancient roots. The interactive format, especially with the responsorial Psalm, encourages active participation from the congregation. It's not just about listening but about engaging with the Word of God together, making it a communal act of worship."

James followed that up with "Lawrence, the format of the readings at Mass is designed to immerse us in the full breadth of God's word, to see the connections between the Old and New Testaments, and to draw us into a deeper relationship with Christ. It's a journey through the history of salvation, bringing the Scriptures to life in our communal worship and personal faith journey."

Posture at Mass – Sit, Stand or Kneel

Lawrence said "Father Matt, thank you for your patience in explaining things so far, but I have to ask this question - Why is it so hard to follow? Should I stand or sit or kneel, should I listen or respond? We don't have that at my church. Who is right?"

Father Matt replied, "Lawrence, I completely understand your concern. The various postures and responses during the Catholic Mass can seem complicated at first, especially if you're not used to them. Some people have joked about the various postures being 'Catholic calisthenics'. However, each action has a purpose and a deep spiritual significance. The different postures and responses in the Catholic Mass might seem overwhelming at first, but they are deeply rooted in our tradition and serve to enhance our worship. Let's break it down together - First, Standing is a posture of respect and readiness. In Scripture, people often stand to pray and to listen to God's word. For example, in Nehemiah 8:5, when Ezra opened the book of the Law, all the people stood up. We stand during the Gospel reading and certain prayers to show reverence and attention."

He continued, "in Luke 24:36, When Jesus appeared to His disciples after the resurrection, they stood in His presence. Standing during the Gospel symbolizes our attentiveness and respect for the words of Christ."

James said "In my deaconate classes, we just learned that sitting is a posture of learning and reflection. We sit during the other readings and the homily to listen attentively and meditate on God's word. That makes sense doesn't in Lawrence?"

Lawrence responded, "another example is in Luke 10:39, where Mary sat at the Lord's feet, listening to His teaching. I guess I didn't think about how sitting allows us to focus and absorb the message being proclaimed."

Father Matt broke in saying, "and kneeling is a posture of humility, penance, and adoration. We kneel during the Eucharistic Prayer to show our deep reverence for the mystery of Christ's actual presence in the Eucharist. For Paul says in Philippians 2:10, 'At the name of Jesus every knee should bow, in heaven and on earth and under the earth.' Kneeling expresses our worship and submission to God."

Father continued, "The Mass is a communal act of worship, not a passive event. The responses and prayers we say together, like the "Amen" or the "Our Father," are ways for us to actively participate in the liturgy. This active participation helps us to engage more fully with the celebration of the Eucharist. Like in Romans 12:1, St Paul urges us to 'offer your bodies as a living sacrifice, holy and pleasing to God—this is your true and proper worship.' Our physical participation with our postures and responses is part of offering ourselves in worship."

James explains, "These postures and responses unify us as a community. When we stand, sit, kneel, and speak together, we are expressing our unity in the Body of Christ. It is a visible sign that we are one in our faith and in our worship of God."

Lawrence interjects, "In Acts 2:42, it says 'They devoted themselves to the apostles' teaching and to fellowship, to the breaking of bread and to prayer." I guess the early Christians worshiped together in a structured way, reflecting unity and shared devotion in the same way Catholics do."

Fathe Matt speaks up and says, "The structure of the Mass and its various elements have developed over centuries, rooted in Scripture and the practices of the early Church. These traditions help to deepen our faith and connect us to the universal Church. In fact, Paul says in Hebrews 12:1 'We are surrounded by a great cloud of witnesses.' The traditions of the Mass connect us to generations of believers who have worshiped in this way, enriching our spiritual heritage."

Lawrence said, "I can see how the different postures and responses allow us to engage on multiple levels—physically, mentally, and spiritually. They help us to be more mindful and present during the Mass, allowing us to connect with God and with each other in a deeper way. That is a good thing!"

Father followed up with a response "Lawrence, the various elements of the Mass, including standing, sitting, kneeling, listening, and responding, are all designed to bring us into a fuller and more active participation in our worship. It may seem complicated at first, but with time, it becomes a natural and meaningful way to engage with the liturgy."

Father continued, "Who is right? It's not so much about right or wrong but about different traditions expressing their love and reverence for God in ways that are meaningful to them. The Catholic tradition, with its rich liturgical practices, offers a profound way to experience the mystery of faith. I hope this helps you see the beauty and purpose behind these practices."

Priests and Deacons – Roles and Vestments

Lawrence continues "Thanks Father for that explanation. I noticed that when the man people called Deacon Brian finished reading the Gospel, You got up and explained what the readings meant. You and the deacon had the really fancy, decorative robes on. Apparently, everyone has a specific role during the Mass and only priests and deacons were the special robes?"

Father said "Yes, Lawrence, you're absolutely right. The roles during the Mass and the specific vestments worn by priests and deacons are both deeply significant and rooted in the history and traditions of the Church. Each element serves a purpose and reflects our reverence for the sacred liturgy. Let's break down the significance of these roles and the special robes, known as vestments."

James said, "I can cover the deacon part - The deacon has a unique role in the Mass. Deacons assist the priest and are ordained for service. They proclaim the Gospel, can preach the homily, assist at the altar, and sometimes lead certain prayers. Their role is to serve both the liturgy and the community."

James continued "in Acts 6:2-4, it states that the apostles appointed deacons to serve the community so that they could focus on prayer and the ministry of the word. This established the deacon's role of service and assistance in the early Church."

Father Matt shared, "The priest's primary role at Mass is to celebrate the Eucharist, consecrate the bread and wine, and lead the community in worship. The priest acts in the person of Christ, in Latin, you will hear the phrase in 'persona Christi', during the Mass, especially during the Eucharistic Prayer. Outside of Mass, in the confessional, it is Jesus, acting through the priest, who is actually absolving you of your sins". In 1 Corinthians 11:24-25, Paul recounts Jesus' words at the Last Supper, which the priest repeats during the consecration – 'This is my body, do this in remembrance of me.' The priest, acting in the person of Christ, makes this sacrificial act present during the Mass."

James said, "Vestments are not just fancy robes; they have deep symbolic meaning and help to set apart the liturgical celebration from everyday life. They remind us that the priest and deacon are serving in a special, sacred role. Father, could you share the names and meanings of each of the vestments?"

Father Matt said "The Alb is a long white robe worn by both priests and deacons. It symbolizes purity and baptism. White is the color of baptism, representing the new life we receive in Christ. In Revelation 7:9, John describes a vision of a great multitude standing before the throne of God, wearing white robes, symbolizing purity and victory.

He continues, "The stole is a long, narrow strip of cloth worn by priests and deacons. For priests, it hangs around the neck and down the front. For deacons, it is worn over the left shoulder and fastened at the right side. The stole symbolizes the yoke of Christ and the authority of the ordained ministry. For in Matthew 11:29-30, Jesus says, 'Take my yoke upon you and learn from me, for I am gentle and humble in heart.' The stole reminds us of the servant leadership that Christ exemplified."

Father continues to say, "The chasuble is the outermost garment worn by the priest. It symbolizes the love and charity of Christ, which covers all. Its color changes with the liturgical seasons; green for Ordinary Time, purple for Advent and Lent, white for Christmas and Easter. Paul writes in Colossians 3:14, 'And over all these virtues put on love, which binds them all together in perfect unity.' The chasuble represents this garment of love."

James speaks up, "The dalmatic is a vestment similar to the chasuble but with sleeves, and is worn by deacons. It represents joy and service. The design and color often match the priest's chasuble, symbolizing unity in their roles during the Mass."

Father explains "The specific roles during the Mass, from the priest and deacon to the lectors and altar servers, highlight the communal nature of our worship. Each person's participation, whether in a specific role or in the congregation, contributes to the fullness of the liturgical celebration. Paul explains in 1 Corinthians 12:4-6, 'There are different kinds of gifts, but the same Spirit distributes them. There are different kinds of service, but the same Lord.' Each role and service in the Mass reflects the diversity of gifts within the Body of Christ."

Father expounds a little more, "Lawrence, the roles and vestments you noticed are integral to our worship. They emphasize the sacred nature of the liturgy and the specific vocations within the Church. The priest and deacon's vestments remind us, and them, of their special roles in serving the community and leading us in the celebration of the Eucharist. I hope this explanation helps you see the beauty and purpose behind these traditions, enriching your understanding of the Mass."

The Creed

Father Matt shared, "Getting back to the Mass, the next thing we profess is the Creed. While the content of the creeds is largely the same across traditions, the theological emphasis can differ. Catholic interpretation of the Creed is deeply intertwined with the teachings of the Church Fathers, the Magisterium which is the teaching authority of the Church, and centuries of theological development. Protestant and evangelical interpretations might emphasize personal faith and direct Scriptural understanding, often with less or no reliance on ecclesiastical tradition."

Father explains, "For Catholics, the Creed is part of a broader liturgical and sacramental tradition. It is professed within the context of the Mass, reinforcing the connection between faith and the Eucharist. It is my understanding that for many Protestant and evangelical communities, the Creed serves as a concise summary of faith but is not necessarily tied to liturgical practice in the same way."

Father concludes his explanation of the Creed, "Lawrence, the Nicene and Apostles' Creeds are profound statements of Christian faith originated centuries before the major Protestant denominations were created but are now shared by many denominations, including Catholics and various Protestant traditions. The differences lie more in emphasis, tradition, and liturgical practice rather than in the fundamental truths they profess. The creeds serve to unite Christians in the core beliefs of our faith, even as we express and live out these beliefs in diverse ways. I hope this helps you see how the profession of faith functions in the Catholic Church and how it connects us to the broader Christian tradition."

Prayer of the Faithful

James unfolds the purpose of the next step in the Mass, "Lawrence, the Prayer of the Faithful is an important part of the Catholic Mass. It's a time when the congregation offers prayers for the needs of the Church, the world, those in need, and the local community. Let's take a closer look at how this prayer functions in the Catholic Church and compare it to practices in Protestant services."

James continues, "In the Catholic Mass, the Prayer of the Faithful follows the homily and the Creed. It's a series of intercessions where the congregation prays for various intentions. These typically include - The needs of the Church; Public authorities and the salvation of the world; Those burdened by any kind of difficulty; The local community and the faithful departed. "

Father explains, "This is rooted in 1 Timothy 2:1-2 as Paul writes, 'I urge, then, first of all, that petitions, prayers, intercession and thanksgiving be made for all people—for kings and all those in authority, that we may live peaceful and quiet lives in all godliness and holiness.' This passage underscores the biblical basis for praying for various needs and authorities."

He continues, "You may not recognize the specific structure of the Prayer of the Faithful present in every Protestant denomination, but many have similar practices of intercessory prayer. In many Protestant traditions, the pastor leads a pastoral prayer during the service. This prayer often includes intercessions for the congregation, the community, and broader concerns, similar to the Catholic Prayer of the Faithful."

Lawrence chimed in and said, "In mine and some other evangelical and charismatic churches we have times of open prayer where members of the congregation can offer prayers aloud. This can be spontaneous and reflect the needs and concerns of those present. The problem is some people have a litany of every relative and their relative's friends"

Lawrence continued, "In more liturgical Protestant denominations, such as Anglican, Lutheran, and some Reformed churches, I learned as a teenager that there are structured prayers and litanies that closely resemble what I saw at today's Catholic Prayer of the Faithful. These prayers follow a similar pattern of intercession for the Church, the world, and specific needs."

James added "The theological emphasis behind these prayers is generally consistent across traditions: to bring before God the needs and concerns of the community and the world, recognizing our dependence on His grace and mercy. In James 5:16 it says 'Therefore confess your sins to each other and pray for each other so that you may be healed. The prayer of a righteous person is powerful and effective.' This highlights the power of communal prayer and intercession."

Father Matt concluded the discussion, "Lawrence, while the form and structure of intercessory prayers may vary among Protestant denominations, the practice of praying for the needs of the Church, the community, and the world is a common thread. In the Catholic Mass, this takes the form of the Prayer of the Faithful, a structured series of intercessions that involve the entire congregation. In Protestant services, this might be reflected in pastoral prayers, congregational prayers, or set litanies, all aimed at lifting up the needs of the faithful and the world to God."

He continued with, "I hope this helps you see the commonalities and differences in how our traditions approach intercessory prayer, all rooted in a shared desire to seek God's help and guidance in our lives and the lives of others. The next part of the Mass is called the Liturgy of the Eucharist. I am sure you will have a few questions about that."

The Liturgy of the Eucharist
The Presentation of the Gifts in the Mass

Lawrence asks Father Matt "After the prayers of the Faithful, a family left their seats and walked toward the back of the church and collected gifts of the communion wafer and wine and then processed up the aisle and gave them to you in front of the altar. Why the formality for ordinary things?"

Father replied "When the family brings forward the bread and wine, they represent the whole community offering these gifts to God. It is a symbolic gesture where we present not just these physical elements but also our lives, our work, and our intentions. This act of bringing forward the gifts prepares them for the Eucharistic Prayer, where they will be consecrated and transformed into the Body and Blood of Christ."

Father Matt continued, "But Lawrence, that's a very insightful question. The Presentation of the Gifts, or the Offertory, is a meaningful part of the Catholic Mass that, as I just mentioned, involves the congregation in a tangible way. This is more than just a formality; it has deep scriptural and historical roots that connect us to the traditions of the early Church and to the broader biblical narrative. The Presentation of the Gifts is a profound moment in the Mass where we bring forward the bread and wine that will become the Body and Blood of Christ during the Consecration. The act of the Presentation is rich in symbolism and rooted in Scripture, reflecting our participation in the sacrificial offering. Let me explain using some key scriptural references for the significance of the bread and wine in this context."

The Significance of Bread

FATHER MATT CONTINUED, "In Sirach 29:21, it states 'The necessities of life are water, bread, clothing, and a house to assure privacy.' This passage highlights bread as a basic necessity, symbolizing sustenance and life. In offering bread, we present something fundamental to our existence," adding, "In Sirach 39:26-27 it says, 'Basic necessities for human life are water and fire, iron and salt, the heart of wheat, milk and honey, the blood of the grape, oil, and clothing.' Here, bread, the heart of wheat, is listed among essential items, indicating its importance in daily life and its symbolic value in religious rituals.

"Jacob offered a sacrifice on the mountain and invited his kinsmen to the meal. They ate the meal and spent the night on the mountain." Father quoted Genesis 31:54. In this passage, bread is part of a communal meal associated with sacrifice and covenant, prefiguring the Eucharistic meal.

A few chapters later, in Genesis 37:25, it says, "As they sat down to eat their meal, they looked up and saw a caravan of Ishmaelites coming from Gilead. Their camels were loaded with spices, balm, and myrrh, and they were on their way to take them down to Egypt." This verse, while not directly about bread, sets the scene for a communal meal, hinting at the importance of shared meals in biblical narratives.

The Significance of Wine

FATHER CONTINUED IN explaining the wine, "In Psalm 104:15, it states, 'Wine to gladden the heart of man, oil to make his face shine, and bread to strengthen man's heart.' This verse highlights wine as a source of joy and a complement to bread, emphasizing the celebratory and life-giving aspects of both elements."

Then in Sirach 31:27, Father explains, "'Wine is very life to human beings if taken in moderation. What is life to one who is without wine? It has been created to make people happy.' Wine is seen as a gift from

God that brings joy and festivity, aligning with its use in celebrations and sacrifices."

Father said, "Later in Sirach 39:26-27, the same passage that mentions bread also lists wine, as 'the blood of the grape' as a basic necessity, underscoring its importance in both daily life and religious observance."

In summary, the Presentation of the Gifts is not just about moving items from one place to another; it's a deeply symbolic action that connects us to the scriptural heritage and the mystery of the Eucharist. The bread and wine, simple yet profound symbols of sustenance and joy, are offered to become the Sacramental presence of Christ among us. This ritual reminds us of our call to bring our lives and offerings to God, trusting in His transformative power.

Washing of Hands

Father explained "Lawrence, the ritual of the washing of hands during the Mass is a significant and ancient tradition with deep biblical and theological roots. It's a gesture of purification and preparation that echoes various scriptural practices and symbolizes the priest's readiness to offer the holy sacrifice of the Mass. Let me explain how this ritual connects to our scriptural heritage and the sacred duties of the priest."

Father continued, "In Psalm 24:3-4, David said 'Who may ascend the mountain of the Lord? Who may stand in his holy place? The one who has clean hands and a pure heart, who does not trust in an idol or swear by a false god.' This psalm speaks to the necessity of purity for those who enter God's presence. The act of washing hands symbolizes the priest's desire for internal purity as he prepares to perform the sacred rites."

Father says, "Later, in Psalm 26:6-7, it says 'I wash my hands in innocence, and go about your altar, Lord, proclaiming aloud your praise and telling of all your wonderful deeds.' Here, the psalmist associates the washing of hands with innocence and purity before approaching the altar. This verse highlights the connection between physical cleansing and spiritual readiness to participate in worship and sacrifice."

Father then explains the Role of Priests in the Old Testament, citing Exodus 30:18-21, which says, "Make a bronze basin, with its bronze stand, for washing. Place it between the tent of meeting and the altar, and put water in it. Aaron and his sons are to wash their hands and feet with water from it. Whenever they enter the tent of meeting, they shall wash with water so that they will not die. Also, when they approach the altar to minister by presenting a food offering to the Lord, they shall wash their hands and feet so that they will not die. This ritual purification was essential for their service and to avoid defilement. It underscores the seriousness and sanctity of their duties, a theme that carries into our liturgical practices today.

Father said, "Now, let's get into the Theological Significance of the Washing of Hands in the Mass. In the Catechism of the Catholic Church, CCC 1366, it states that 'The Eucharist is thus a sacrifice because it re-presents, or makes present, the sacrifice of the cross, because it is its memorial and because it applies its fruit.'

He continued, "The washing of hands symbolizes the priest's preparation to offer this sacrifice. Just as the priests of the Old Testament purified themselves before offering sacrifices, the priest today washes his hands to signify his own spiritual preparation and purity before consecrating the Eucharist."

James explained "in John 13:4-5 and 12-14, it states 'So he got up from the meal, took off his outer clothing, and wrapped a towel around his waist. After that, he poured water into a basin and began to wash his disciples' feet, drying them with the towel that was wrapped around him. When he had finished washing their feet, he put on his clothes and returned to his place. 'Do you understand what I have done for you?' he asked them. 'You call me "Teacher" and "Lord," and rightly so, for that is what I am. Now that I, your Lord and Teacher, have washed your feet, you also should wash one another's feet.'"

James continued, "Although this passage refers to the washing of feet rather than hands, it highlights the importance of humility and purification in service. Jesus' act of washing the disciples' feet demonstrates a model of servanthood and purity that the priest embodies when he washes his hands before the Eucharist."

Father concluded, "Lawrence, the washing of hands during the Mass is ritual rich in meaning and history. It is not merely about cleanliness but symbolizes the priest's spiritual purification and readiness to enter into the sacred act of offering the Eucharistic sacrifice. This practice links us to the traditions of the Old Testament priests and the teachings of Jesus, reminding us of the purity and devotion required to stand before God and serve His people. This gesture is a humble acknowledgment of the need for God's grace and purification as we approach the holy mysteries of our faith."

The Eucharistic Prayer

Father Matt said, "Lawrence, the Eucharistic Prayer is the heart of the Mass, where we enter into the mystery of Christ's sacrifice, joining our prayers with the heavenly liturgy. It is a moment when heaven and earth meet, and we participate in the eternal sacrifice of Christ."

He continued, "This prayer encompasses several parts, including the Preface, the "Holy, Holy, Holy" (Sanctus), the Words of Institution, and the Doxology. Each component is deeply rooted in Scripture and Tradition, revealing the profound significance of what we celebrate. Because of its extreme importance, let's explore this further with the help of various scriptural and magisterial sources."

Father held his reference and read, "The first source is the Sacrosanctum Concilium 8: 'In the earthly liturgy we take part in a foretaste of that heavenly liturgy which is celebrated in the holy city of Jerusalem, toward which we journey as pilgrims'. Lawrence, our time here on Earth is only part of the journey of life God Plans for us. We spend a relatively short time here on Earth in a journey toward Eternal Life, hopefully in Heaven. So we really are pilgrims, on our way to Heaven. We must always remember that this is not the destination, but a stop on the journey. Remembering this allows us not to hold tightly to what we have here, but to focus on the final destination. He is waiting patiently for us at the gates of Heaven to give us our reward. But at the same time, He knows that we need food for the way, which is the Eucharist! It gives us physical and spiritual strength."

Father Matt continued, "The first part of the Eucharistic Prayer is the Preface, lifting our hearts to God and giving thanks for His mighty works. It sets the tone of thanksgiving and praise, recognizing God's holiness and the gift of salvation.

Father said, "Recall 'The Holy, Holy, Holy'? We also call it the Sanctus. It mirrors Isaiah's Vision, from Isaiah 6:1-3 'In the year that King Uzziah died, I saw the Lord, high and exalted, seated on a throne; and the train of his robe filled the temple. Above him were seraphim, each with six wings... And they were calling to one another: 'Holy, holy, holy is the Lord Almighty; the whole earth is full of his glory.'"

Clarifying, Father said, "This vision of Isaiah provides the foundation for the Sanctus. The cry of "Holy, Holy, Holy" is an acknowledgment of God's absolute holiness and glory, uniting our earthly liturgy with the worship of the heavenly hosts.

"The Words of Institution are the central part of the Eucharistic Prayer, where the priest repeats Jesus' words from the Last Supper, consecrating the bread and wine as the Body and Blood of Christ."

James said, "Lawrence, remember Luke 22:19-20, where is says, 'And he took bread, gave thanks and broke it, and gave it to them, saying, 'This is my body given for you; do this in remembrance of me.' In the same way, after the supper he took the cup, saying, 'This cup is the new covenant in my blood, which is poured out for you.'" This passage recounts Jesus instituting the Eucharist, commanding His disciples to continue this memorial of His sacrifice.

Father Matt then got into the details, "The concept of sacrifice is integral to understanding the Eucharist. The Eucharistic Prayer reflects the sacrificial nature of Jesus' death and its significance for our salvation."

"In Leviticus 4, this chapter outlines the sin offerings in the Old Testament, prefiguring the ultimate sacrifice of Christ. The detailed instructions for offerings for atonement highlight the importance of sacrifice in the relationship between God and His people."

"In Mark 10:45, 'For even the Son of Man did not come to be served, but to serve, and to give his life as a ransom for many.'"

He continued, "Jesus' self-giving is the ultimate fulfillment of the sacrificial system, offering Himself for our redemption."

"In the Catechism of the Catholic Church 1364, it states 'In the New Testament, the memorial takes on new meaning. When the Church celebrates the Eucharist, she commemorates Christ's Passover, and it is made present: the sacrifice Christ offered once for all on the cross remains ever present.'"

James said, "The Eucharist makes present the one sacrifice of Christ in a sacramental manner, allowing us to participate in its graces."

Father went on, "In the Catechism of the Catholic Church 1366, it says 'The Eucharist is thus a sacrifice because it re-presents, or makes present, the sacrifice of the cross, because it is its memorial and because it applies its fruit.' This teaching emphasizes that the Eucharist is not a repetition but a re-presentation of Christ's unique sacrifice, made accessible to us in every Mass."

James grabbed the bible and said, "Here is the historical context – first in 1 Maccabees 2:49-50, 'Now the days drew near for Mattathias to die, and he said to his sons - Arrogance and scorn have now grown strong; it is a time of ruin and furious anger. Now, my children, show zeal for the law, and give your lives for the covenant of our ancestors.'"

Then, "In 1 Maccabees 6:43-46, This passage recounts the heroic martyrdom of Eleazar, who sacrificed his life for his faith, echoing the self-sacrifice that Jesus would exemplify."

Father said, "The Eucharistic Prayer concludes with the Doxology, a prayer of praise to the Holy Trinity, bringing the prayer to its climax. In 1 Chronicles 16:36, it says Praise be to the Lord, the God of Israel, from everlasting to everlasting. Then all the people said 'Amen' and 'Praise the Lord.' This verse emphasizes the communal aspect of praise and the importance of the people's affirmation.

Then, he said "in Nehemiah 8:6 it says 'Ezra praised the Lord, the great God; and all the people lifted their hands and responded, 'Amen! Amen!' Then they bowed down and worshiped the Lord with their faces to the ground.' Here, the people's response of 'Amen' signifies their agreement and participation in the prayer of praise.

And finally, in Revelation 5:13-14, it says "Then I heard every creature in heaven and on earth and under the earth and on the sea, and all that is in them, saying: 'To him who sits on the throne and to the Lamb be praise and honor and glory and power, for ever and ever!' The four living creatures said, 'Amen,' and the elders fell down and worshiped. This passage reflects the heavenly liturgy where all creation joins in the praise of God, mirroring our liturgical celebration."

Fathe Matt said, "St. Augustine, one of the most influential Christian theologians and philosophers of the early Church born in 354 AD, in Tagaste, a Roman province in present-day Algeria, and died on August 28, 430 AD emphasized the power of the 'Amen' said by the congregation. He described it as a strong affirmation of faith and agreement with the prayers offered, signifying the unity of the Church in worship."

He continued, "Lawrence, the Eucharistic Prayer, with its Preface, Sanctus, Words of Institution, and Doxology, draws us into the mystery of Christ's sacrifice. It is deeply rooted in the scriptural traditions of sacrifice, thanksgiving, and holiness. This prayer transforms the bread and wine into the Body and Blood of Christ, making His one sacrifice present to us and inviting us to participate in the heavenly liturgy. Through these sacred actions, we are united with the worship of the angels and saints, and we experience the profound grace of Christ's redemptive love. The people's "Amen" is a powerful affirmation, echoing the praise of all creation and sealing our participation in this sacred mystery."

Fathe Matt explained, "Lawrence, the Communion Rite and the Concluding Rite are the final parts of the Mass, where we prepare our hearts to receive Christ and then are sent forth to live out the Gospel in our daily lives. Each element of these rites is deeply rooted in Scripture and tradition, and they draw us closer to the mystery of Christ's presence in the Eucharist."

James interjected "The Communion Rite begins with the Lord's Prayer, which Jesus taught us. This prayer holds profound significance in our faith. In Galatians 4:4-6 it says 'But when the set time had fully come, God sent his Son, born of a woman, born under the law, to redeem those under the law, that we might receive **adoption to sonship**. Because you are His sons, God sent the Spirit of his Son into our hearts, the Spirit who calls out, 'Abba, Father.' This passage highlights our identity as God's children, which is why we can call Him 'Father.' Then, in 1 John 3:1, it says 'See what great love the Father has lavished on us, that we should be called children of God! And that is what we are!' The Lord's Prayer reminds us of this intimate relationship with God, rooted in His love."

Father Matt said "After the Lord's Prayer, the priest breaks the consecrated Host, symbolizing Christ's body broken for us. As it is written in 1 Corinthians 11:23-26. 'For I received from the Lord what I also passed on to you - The Lord Jesus, on the night he was betrayed, took bread, and when he had given thanks, he broke it and said, 'This is my body, which is for you; do this in remembrance of me.' This passage recalls the Last Supper and the institution of the Eucharist."

The Father recalled "in 1 Corinthians 10:16-17, it says, 'Is not the cup of thanksgiving for which we give thanks a participation in the blood of Christ? And is not the bread that we break a participation in the body of Christ? Because there is one loaf, we, who are many, are one body, for we all share the one loaf.' The breaking of bread signifies our unity in Christ.

Father continued, "The Agnus Dei is sung or recited, acknowledging Jesus as the Lamb of God who takes away the sins of the world. This is from John 1:29, 'John saw Jesus coming toward him and said, Look, the Lamb of God, who takes away the sin of the world!'"

James said, "In Revelation 5:6 it says, 'Then I saw a Lamb, looking as if it had been slain, standing at the center of the throne.' And in 1

Corinthians 5:6-7 it says, 'Get rid of the old yeast, so that you may be a new unleavened batch—as you really are. For Christ, our Passover lamb, has been sacrificed.'"

Father quoted several other verses, "Revelation 7:9-10 states 'After this I looked, and there before me was a great multitude that no one could count, from every nation, tribe, people and language, standing before the throne and before the Lamb.' This will be a great sight for us! And then there is Isaiah 53:7-12 which says 'He was oppressed and afflicted, yet he did not open his mouth; he was led like a lamb to the slaughter.'"

James emphasized "In Exodus 12:46 'it must be eaten inside the house; take none of the meat outside the house. Do not break any of the bones.'

Father jumped in by saying "Jesus, crucified at the sixth hour, fulfills these prophecies, becoming the true Passover Lamb. The use of the hyssop branch, stated clearly in John 19:29, in the crucifixion signifies Jesus as the new Passover Lamb, with the hyssop blanch wiped against His bloodied face linking the Old and New Covenants."

Father said "Then, we move into the actual Holy Communion, The Wedding Feast! Receiving the Eucharist is a foretaste of the heavenly banquet. In Revelation 19:9, it states that 'Then the angel said to me, Write this - Blessed are those who are invited to the wedding supper of the Lamb!' This verse speaks of the ultimate union with Christ in heaven, which we anticipate in the Eucharist."

James reverently said, "This is when we say 'Lord, I Am Not Worthy...' Before receiving Communion, we express our humility, echoing the words of the centurion from Matthew 8:8, 'The centurion replied, 'Lord, I do not deserve to have you come under my roof. But just say the word, and my servant will be healed.' In the Mass, we say, 'Lord, I am not worthy that you should enter under my roof, but only say the word and my soul shall be healed.' This refers to the roof of our mouth, emphasizing our unworthiness but also Christ's power to heal our venial sins per CCC 1385.

Lawrence commented, "I noticed the bread and wine during the Mass, which reminded me of the Last Supper. How does this tie into Jewish traditions? Sorry I don't know much about Jewish Traditions"

Father Matt replied, "Excellent observation. Don't worry about not knowing or understanding Jewish Traditions or History. The bread and wine used in the Mass are central elements that harken back to the Jewish Passover. In Exodus 12, we see that during Passover, a lamb was sacrificed, bread was broken, and wine was shared. At the Last Supper, Jesus, a devout Jew, celebrated Passover with His disciples, but He gave it a new meaning. He took the bread and wine and said, 'This is my body' and 'This is my blood' in Luke 22:19-20, transforming the Passover meal into what we now call the Eucharist.

Lawrence questioned, "So, the Eucharist is more than just a remembrance?"

Father Matt replied, "Exactly. The Eucharist is a participation in Jesus' sacrifice. Just as the Jews sacrificed an unblemished lamb during Passover in Exodus 12:5, Jesus, the Lamb of God in John 1:29, was sacrificed for our sins. His words at the Last Supper and His death on the cross fulfill the Jewish sacrificial system, especially the Passover."

Lawrence continued his questioning, "What about the significance of bread and wine in Jewish tradition? Is there more to it?"

Father Matt replied, "Yes, indeed. In Jewish tradition, especially as detailed in Leviticus 24:5-9, there is something called the Bread of the Presence, or literally, the 'Bread of the Face.' This bread was kept in the Ark of the Covenant and later, the Temple, signifying God's presence. It was accompanied by wine and consumed by priests every Sabbath. Rabbinic tradition even suggests that this bread underwent a special change once it was consecrated to God. This prefigures the Catholic belief that the bread and wine become the Body and Blood of Christ during the Mass, as Jesus said it was."

Lawrence said, "That's fascinating. I also read about how Jesus' crucifixion aligns with the Jewish temple rituals. Can you elaborate more about that?"

Father Matt answered, "Certainly. During Passover, thousands of lambs were sacrificed in the Temple, and their blood was poured out, symbolizing purification which is directly from Leviticus 16:15-19. This imagery is powerful in the context of Jesus' crucifixion. When Jesus' side was pierced on the cross, water and blood flowed from His side as written in John 19:34, echoing the cleansing of the Temple. Jesus referred to Himself as the New Temple in John 2:19-21, indicating that His body is where God dwells and where ultimate sacrifice and purification occur.

Lawrence asked, "How does the Mass relate to the practices in the Old Testament Temple?"

Father Matt replied, "In the Old Testament, the Temple was the place of sacrifice and worship in 2 Chronicles 7:12-16. The sacrifices, especially during Passover, were a foreshadowing of Christ's sacrifice. The Mass is seen as a continuation of this, but in a fulfilled form. Hebrews 9:11-12 explains that Christ entered the greater and more perfect tabernacle, not made with hands, to offer His own body and blood for our redemption. The Mass commemorates this eternal sacrifice, bringing it into the present for believers to participate in."

Lawrence still searching for answers he could understand asked, "And what about the bread and wine becoming Christ's body and blood? Is there a scriptural basis for this belief?"

Father Matt quickly responded "Yes, there is. Jesus Himself said, 'I am the bread of life' in John 6:35 and later, 'For my flesh is true food, and my blood is true drink' in John 6:55. At the Last Supper, He instituted the Eucharist, saying, 'This is my body given for you; do this in remembrance of me' in Luke 22:19 and similarly with the cup of wine, 'This cup is the new covenant in my blood, which is poured out for you' in Luke 22:20. St. Paul also affirms this in 1 Corinthians 10:16-17, where he speaks about the bread and wine being a participation in the body and blood of Christ."

Lawrence said, "This is incredibly enriching. It's like seeing the Old and New Testaments come together in a living tradition."

Father Matt said, "That's a beautiful way to put it. Understanding these connections helps us appreciate the depth and richness of the Mass. It's a divine participation that transcends time, linking us to the ancient roots of our faith and bringing us into communion with God."

Lawrence asks another question, "One more thing, I read about the Bread of the Presence being shown to pilgrims. How does this relate to the Mass?"

Father Matt replied, "Another good question! The Bread of the Presence was shown to pilgrims during Jewish festivals as a sign of God's love in Exodus 25:30. In the Mass, the Eucharist is our Bread of the Presence. When the priest elevates the consecrated host, it's a moment of profound significance where the host becomes the Body, Blood, Soul and Divinity of Jesus, therefore showing Christ to the faithful and reminding us of God's enduring love and presence among us."

Lawrence thanked Father Matt and James saying "This has given me a lot to reflect on and a deeper appreciation for the Mass."

Father Matt graciously responded, "You're very welcome. I'm glad we could help. If you ever have any more questions or want to discuss further, feel free to reach out. But if you have a few more minutes, there are a few things left about the Eucharist we should cover to tie up any loose strings that are out there."

Father continued, "In the General Instruction of the Roman Missal, 73, it states that 'At the beginning of the Liturgy of the Eucharist, the gifts which will become Christ's Body and Blood are brought to the altar. The offerings are then placed on the altar, and the Eucharistic Prayer begins.' This instruction underscores the transition from presenting ordinary elements to their consecration as sacred. If the family bring up the offertory gifts were to trip and the bread hosts fall to the floor, they would be quickly cleaned up and disposed of and replaced with fresh hosts. After the Consecration, if what appears as nothing different than the hosts dropped before they made it to the altar were to fall from the fingers of the priest as they distribute Holy Communion, that host, being the True Body of Christ would be placed into a special container within the Tabernacle filled with Holy Water and monitored daily until it is completely dissolved."

Father continued, "You may have heard of the many 'Eucharistic Miracles', where the host placed in water in the locked tabernacle of various Catholic Churches around the world never dissolved, but turned bloody, type AB blood in each case. The material around the undissolved host which was bloodied has been determined to be flesh from a human heart, and the flesh has been determined by multiple scientists and doctors to be from a man who had been tortured to death."

Father also shared that in Melchizedek's Offering, Genesis 14:18, "Then Melchizedek, King of Salem, brought out bread and wine. He was priest of God Most High." Melchizedek's offering of bread and wine is seen as a prefiguration of the Eucharist. Jesus is considered a priest in the order of Melchizedek, linking this Old Testament event to the Last Supper and the Catholic Mass.

Further, Father Matt said that The Last Supper, Matthew 26:26-28 states, "While they were eating, Jesus took bread, and when he had given thanks, he broke it and gave it to his disciples, saying, 'Take and eat; this is my body.' Then he took a cup, and when he had given thanks, he gave it to them, saying, 'Drink from it, all of you. This is my blood of the covenant, which is poured out for many for the forgiveness of sins.'" This passage directly connects the elements of bread and wine to Jesus' sacrifice and the establishment of the New Covenant.

Concluding Rite

Father said, Lawrence, the last thing at Mass, the Concluding Rite, sends us forth to live out the Gospel. After Communion, we offer a final prayer of thanksgiving, followed by the blessing and dismissal. The priest or deacon, vested in liturgical garments, sends us with a mission to be Christ's witnesses in the world.

Father said "Lawrence, the Communion Rite and Concluding Rite encapsulate the depth of our faith, from the Lord's Prayer and the breaking of bread to the Agnus Dei and receiving the Eucharist. Each part is steeped in Scripture and tradition, drawing us into the mystery of Christ's sacrifice and our call to live as His disciples. As we receive Christ, we are transformed and sent forth to bring His love to the world.

A Farewell and a Promise

The late afternoon sun cast a warm, golden hue over the grounds of the church as Father Matt, James, and Lawrence walked together toward Lawrence's car in the parking lot. The air was filled with the soft sounds of birds singing their afternoon songs and the gentle rustle of leaves in the breeze. It was a peaceful moment, the kind that made goodbyes feel both bittersweet and hopeful.

Father Matt walked with a calm grace, his hands folded behind his back, while James and Lawrence strolled alongside, their steps in sync. The path to the parking lot was lined with blooming flowers, their vibrant colors a reminder of the beauty and renewal that faith brought to their lives.

As they reached the parking lot, Father Matt turned to Lawrence with a warm smile. "Lawrence, it has been a blessing to have you with us these past days. Your presence and questions has enriched us, and your journey has reminded us of our own."

Lawrence smiled back, a mixture of gratitude and sadness in his eyes. "Thank you, Father Matt. Being here has been a gift. I've learned so much and felt so welcomed."

Father Matt placed a gentle hand on Lawrence's shoulder. "Remember, Lawrence, that Catholics, like all Christians, are imperfect models of Christ in an imperfect world. We strive, we falter, and we rise again, always with the help of God's grace."

James nodded in agreement, his eyes reflecting the sincerity of Father Matt's words. "We're all on this journey together, Lawrence. We're called to love and support each other, just as Christ loves us."

Father Matt continued, his voice steady and reassuring. "As brothers with Christ, we are called to walk this path together, helping one another, forgiving one another, and lifting each other up. Our journey to the promised land is not one we undertake alone. We do it in community, in faith, and in love."

Lawrence took a deep breath, feeling the weight and comfort of their words. "I'll carry that with me. This community, this faith—it's something I'll never forget. I hope to return someday, to walk with you all again."

Father Matt's eyes twinkled with a hint of pride and hope. "You'll always be welcome here, Lawrence. Our doors are open, and our hearts are with you, wherever your journey takes you."

James stepped forward, extending his hand. "Take care, my brother. We'll be praying for you."

Lawrence shook James's hand firmly, then embraced him. "And I for you. Thank you, James, for everything."

As Lawrence stepped back, Father Matt offered a final blessing. "May the Lord bless you and keep you. May His face shine upon you and be gracious to you. May He lift up His countenance upon you and give you peace."

Lawrence bowed his head, accepting the blessing with a full heart. "Amen."

With one last look at the rectory, the church, and the friends he had made, Lawrence turned and drove away, feeling a sense of peace and purpose. He knew that wherever his path led, he carried with him the love and support of this community, and the enduring promise of faith.

As Father Matt and James watched him go, they stood in silent prayer, grateful for the time they had shared and hopeful for the journeys yet to come. The sun dipped lower, casting long shadows that seemed to stretch towards the horizon, a reminder that every ending was but a new beginning.

The church bells rang out, their sound a gentle call to father's evening prayers. Father Matt said good evening to James as he got into his car, then turned back towards the sanctuary, ready to welcome the next chapter of their own journeys, knowing that they, too, were imperfect models of Christ, striving together towards the promised land.

Also by John H Brennan

Thru The First Disciple's Eyes
Thru the First Disciple's Eyes
Through the Eyes of the Disciple Jesus Loved
Through the Eyes of Cleopas

Standalone
Advice From Above
The Rosary Revealed
Yes, I Knew!
Through The Eyes of Longinus
From Questions to Communion: Discovering Catholicism

About the Author

John is a cradle Catholic, the middle child of five, who grew up in upstate New York. Vatican Two saved him from learning Latin the year he trained to be an Altar Server. He attended Catholic School until High School when he transitioned to public school. He received two associates degrees from the local Community College, then started a job in a fortune 500 company as a draftsman. He had met the woman of his dreams and they had the first of their children 9 months after they were married. Six months later, the three headed off to the State University of New York at Buffalo where John studied Mechanical Engineering. By the time John graduated with his BS in Mechanical Engineering, they had their second son and headed back to his hometown to continue his 40 year career and have a third son and finally his daughter. He and his wife now have a son in law, a daughter in law and six beautiful grandchildren. Several events led him to deepen his faith – joining a Catholic Men's Bible Study; attending several Catholic Men's Conferences; attending a Catholic Men's Emmaus Retreat as well as being on several Emmaus Retreat Teams (including giving witness talks); attending daily Mass; Praying the Holy Rosary daily and being an Extraordinary Minister of Holy Communion at Church and Nursing Homes in the area. His engineering job brought him across the USA as well as Mexico, Europe and Asia where he enjoyed creating his own personal Pilgrimages to Holy Sites and sharing the experiences and pictures with family and friends. His retirement ambitions include enjoying his children and grandchildren, continued travel to holy sites around the world and sharing his Catholic faith wherever he can.